MW01593600

A HEARTFELT MESSAGE TO CHERISH FOREVER

SIGNATURE:

WARNING

Enter at Your Own Risk of Permanent Cringe!

INTRODUCTION

Hey there, folks! You're holding in your hands the ultimate dad joke book, specially crafted for the occasion of Father's Day. I'm here to tell you that this book is filled to the brim with knee-slappers, chuckle-inducers, and of course, those groan-worthy puns that make you wonder if dads are born with a unique sense of humor.

This book is designed to be the perfect gift for the amazing dads out there who never miss an opportunity to crack a joke or lighten up the mood. It's meant to be enjoyed by the whole family, from the youngest to the oldest. So, gather 'round, and let's embark on a laughter-filled journey together.

These dad jokes are divided into different themes, so you'll find a little something for everyone. Whether it's technology, travel, or just the everyday occurrences that make life interesting, these jokes are sure to strike a chord with dads and families alike.

But wait, there's more! We've added a bonus section with tips for nailing dad joke delivery, so you won't bomb at family gatherings and unite the whole family.
So, what are you waiting for?

TABLE OF CONTENT

⌐ BONUS CONTENT ¬

The Ultimate Dad Joke Delivery Guide

103

Timing is Everything

104

The Art of the Eye Roll

105

Confidence is Key

WE ONLY LIVE ONCE !

THE QUINTESSENTIAL ! GUIDE TO DAD JOKES THAT GUARANTEE ONE-TIME LAUGHTER OR LIFETIME EMBARRASSMENT.

Can you tell me why the Statue of Liberty stands in New York Harbor?

Because she can't sit *down!*

. . . .

Why don't you wear snow boots?

Because they will melt.

. . . .

A skunk was arrested for counterfeiting.

Apparently, he gave out bad scents.

What did the cactus say when it was accused of being prickly?

I'm just a little sharp around the edges.

Son, I've lost my keys. Son:

Don't worry, dad, they're always in the last place you look.

I got promoted to head chef in my house. My signature dish?

Cereal, no milk.

What did the football say to the soccer ball?

'You can't play with me, you're not my type!

What's a scarecrow's favorite type of music?

Hay-seed roll!

What would you do if a plate falls on you?

Break down.

'Gone with the Wind' is my most cherished film.

It really blew me away.

I've started gardening, and I'm really digging it.

I just can't seem to root out all the weeds.

Why don't movies make good cooks?

Because they always spoil the broth.

What's the coolest place to bring a jacket?

Alaska.

Why did the hairbrush never lose at poker?

It always goes straight to the root.

Doctor, I think I need glasses.

Doctor: "You certainly do, sir, this is a bakery.

I've become an expert in home improvement...

by knowing exactly where the duct tape is.

What's the term for a cat who does magic tricks?

A purr-cadabra!

What do you call a bicycle that can't stand up by itself?

Two-tired.

Why did the snow globe get a promotion?

Because it always shakes things up.

. . . .

My kids asked me what a solar eclipse is.

I said, it's no big deal, it just throws a little shade.

. . . .

I started a new workout routine.

It involves lifting...the TV remote.

. . . .

Why was the book a great politician?

Because it always had a good spine.

. . . .

Why did the sunglasses go to school?

To get some class.

What do you do when a backpack starts to cry?

You comfort it and say it's all 'zipped' up.

Why don't I trust that tree?

It seems a bit shady.

I decided to take up painting...

my house's fence.

What did the dad wallet say to the kid wallet?

Keep your cents to yourself.

What do you call a watch that doesn't tell time?

A waste of time.

Why did the camera get an award?

It was always in the 'picture'.

Son, why is your sister named Rose?

Because your mother loves roses. Thanks, Dad. No problem, BBQ Ribs.

I mastered a new instrument...

the barbecue grill.

Why was the guitar always on time?

It always kept a good tempo.

Why was the tennis racket a great musician?

It had perfect string control.

What will be your reaction sunglasses walks up to you?

Just 'shade' it off.

My TV show is 'The Walking Dead.'

It reminds me of me before my morning coffee.

I've become a financial advisor...

for my kids' allowance.

Why was the tennis racket so bad at making decisions?

It always gets strung along.

Why was the compass so good at making decisions?

It always knows where it's heading.

Why did the bathrobe get a timeout?

It always wraps things up too soon.

Doctor, I think I'm a moth. Why did you come into the kitchen?

I saw the light.

I've started doing magic tricks. My best one yet?

Making chocolate disappear in seconds.

Why was the pillow so good at secrets?

It always keeps things under cover.

Why did the wallet join the circus?

It loves to flip and 'fold'.

My kids asked me if I could put the cat out.

I didn't know it was on fire.

I've become an expert in fashion.

I can pick the right sweatpants for any occasion.

Why was the coffee mug so funny?

It always cracks everyone up.

Why was the wristwatch so good at school?

It always knew the 'hour' of the day.

Why was the oven mitt always content?

It always feels 'warm' inside.

Why don't I trust stairs?

They're always up to something or leading me down.

I've picked up a new hobby - singing.

I'm great at solo performances, especially when I'm alone.

Why was the umbrella always the hero?

It always covers for everyone.

Why did the pencil sharpener go to therapy?

It couldn't handle the point anymore.

What do you call a camera that's tired of taking pictures?

'Shuttered' down.

Doctor, I think I've become a refrigerator.

Well, you do seem to be keeping things cool.

I've started a gardening hobby,

specializing in growing belly button lint.

Why was the pillow proud?

Because it was cushioning everyone's dreams.

What do you call a wristwatch that only works in the sun?

A sundial.

Why was the backpack always stressed?

It always carries a lot of 'baggage'.

My favorite TV show is 'Friends.'

It reminds me of the imaginary ones I had as a child.

Why did the guitar give a lecture?

Because it had a lot of pluck.

I've decided to start a career in photography. My favorite model?

The fridge, it never blinks.

Why did the camera become a detective?

It always knew how to focus on the details.

Why did the skipping rope join the circus?

It wanted to 'skip' the line.

Son, why is your brother named Jet?

Because your mother loves jets. Thanks, dad. No problem, Pizza.

. . . .

I've started a fitness routine, lifting weights...

of pizza into my mouth.

. . . .

Why was the oven mitt so popular?

Because it never let anyone get burned.

. . . .

What do you call a tennis racket that keeps falling over?

A trip hazard.

. . . .

Why was the chess board always confident?

It always knew its next move.

My kids asked me to explain what a solar eclipse is.

I said it's just the sun playing hide and seek.

I've taken up painting, my masterpiece?

It's called 'Coffee Stain on White Shirt'.

What did the water bottle say to the coffee mug?

You're too hot-headed!

What do you call a pillow that can sing?

A lullaby.

What do you call a snow globe that's too warm?

Global warming.

Why don't I trust atoms?

Because they make up everything.

. . . .

I've decided to become an astronaut, my mission?

Floating around the house.

. . . .

Why was the tennis racket a great storyteller?

It had a lot of strings to its tale.

. . . .

Why was the compass always the leader?

It knew where to go.

. . . .

Why did the umbrella go to school?

It wanted to be 'under' standing.

I've become a master chef. My specialty?

Scrambled eggs, sunny side up.

Why was the water bottle so popular?

It was always refreshing.

What do you call a guitar that can't play music?

A silent string.

What did the keychain say to the key?

You 'unlock' my heart.

I've taken up the art of camouflage.

It's so effective, I can't even find myself.

Why did the guitar become a gardener?

It had the right pluck for it.

. . . .

What do you call a backpack that's good at math?

A 'pack'tical genius.

. . . .

Why did the lampshade become a comedian?

It wanted to 'lighten' the mood.

. . . .

I've started a new workout routine.

I do a sit-up every morning when I wake up.

. . . .

Why was the coffee mug so good at debates?

It always had strong grounds.

Why did the oven mitts join the boxing team?

They could really take the heat.

· ·

Why did the keychain join a band?

It knew how to 'key' in.

· ·

I've started training for a marathon.

So far, I've made it from the couch to the fridge.

· ·

Why was the umbrella always prepared?

It always kept things under wraps.

· ·

What do you call a wristwatch that doesn't tell time?

A wristband.

Why was the lampshade a great detective?

It knew how to 'shed light' on the situation.

. . . .

I've decided to start a rock band.

We're called 'The Rolling Dad Bods'.

. . . .

Why was the water bottle a great actor?

It always got into the 'role'.

. . . .

What do you call a pillow that loves to travel?

A 'rest'less wanderer.

. . . .

I've become a carpenter. My first project?

Assembling flat-pack furniture.

Why did the compass become a tour guide?

It always points in the right direction.

Why was the guitar always late?

It always got 'caught up' in the strings.

I've taken up bird watching.

It's mostly just pigeons in the parking lot, but still.

Why was the guitar a good listener?

It always got 'plucked' into conversations.

What do you call a snow globe that can predict weather?

A snow-caster.

I've started a new diet where I eat everything with a fork.

Even soup.

· ·

Why was the tennis racket a good teacher?

It always had the right 'swing' of things.

· ·

I've started doing yoga. My favorite pose?

The Couch Potato.

· ·

Why was the coffee mug a great comedian?

It always knew how to 'brew' a joke.

· ·

I've become a master at origami. My specialty?

Folding laundry.

I've taken up mountain climbing. The tallest one so far?

The pile of dishes in my sink.

I've started investing in stocks.

Beef, chicken, vegetable, you name it.

I've become an expert in time travel.

I just close my eyes and it's morning.

I've started training for the Olympics. My event?

The 100-meter dash to the TV remote.

I've become a film director. My masterpiece?

'The Adventures of the Lost Remote Control'.

DAILY EMBARRASSMENTS, I GUESS...

COLLECTION OF DAILY LIFE PUNS ENSURING YOUR FAMILY NEVER FORGETS THEIR DAD'S UNIQUE SENSE OF HUMOR.

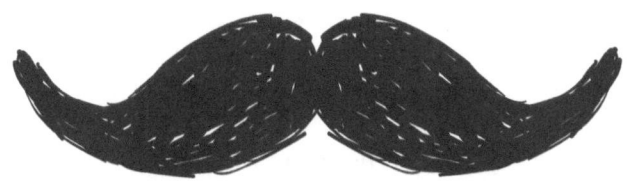

I've tried being a soccer coach. The problem?

I can't even kick a bad habit!

What do diapers say to each other at a party?

"Let's have a poop!"

Tried to be a bedtime story writer.

Quit when I couldn't make it past "Once upon a time..."

What's a soccer player's favorite type of tea?

Penal-tea!

I considered doing my own home repairs.

But I can't even fix a sandwich.

Why did the lawn ask for a bedtime story?

It wanted to hear a grass-roots tale!

I thought about becoming a financial planner.

But I can't even budget my time!

What did the dollar say to the budget planner?

"You're making no cents."

I attempted to learn car maintenance.

But I couldn't even get a grip on the steering wheel.

Why did the car need a day off?

It was too tired!

Thought about being a chef. Turns out,

my best recipe is a recipe for disaster.

What did the homework say to the student?

"I'm done with you!"

What's a football's favorite time of the day?

Kickoff time!

I tried to coach swimming lessons,

but I couldn't even float a theory!

. . . .

What did the coffee cup say to the alarm clock?

Brew-tiful morning, isn't it?

. . . .

What would you do if a coffee cup runs after you?

Espresso yourself!

. . . .

What happens when a lawn gets promoted?

It becomes a yard!

. . . .

What's a homework's favorite type of music?

Pop quiz!

What happens when a car doesn't believe in itself?

It can't excel!

What's a doctor's favorite type of note?

A patient one!

What would you do if your homework starts singing?

Take note!

Doctor, I can't pay my bills!

Doctor: "Try living on the edge, of your income!"

Teacher, I can't do my homework!

Teacher: "Well, don't let it do you!"

What would you do if your budget starts to shrink?

Stretch your dollars!

·   · · · · · · · · · · · ·

Mom, I can't cook dinner!

Dad: "Well, don't let it cook you!"

·   · · · · · · · · · · · ·

What do you do when your family photo starts to laugh?

Snap out of it!

·   · · · · · · · · · · · ·

What do you call a retirement plan for cars?

A brake!

·   · · · · · · · · · · · ·

Coach, I can't kick the ball!

Dad: "Well, don't let it kick you!"

TECHNOLOGY
IS MY THING

TECH-INSPIRED DAD JOKES THAT'LL MAKE YOUR KIDS WANT TO DISCONNECT FROM THE INTERNET.

What does a laptop do when it gets hot?

It opens Windows!

I've started a new exercise regimen.

My laptop's never been lifted so much.

Why don't cell phones ever get lost?

Because they always have a ring!

I decided to start a career in technology. Now I'm an expert *in hitting 'Ctrl+Z' on Microsoft Word.*

I'm so connected these days, *my TV thinks I'm the remote.*

I've become a sports enthusiast. *I can change sports channels faster than anyone I know!*

What did the Bluetooth say to the headphones? *You're music to my ears!*

I've become a master at multitasking. *I can fail to answer emails and ignore notifications at the same time.*

Why did the smartphone go to school?

Because it wanted to have better 'cell' coverage!

I thought about becoming a video call operator.

I've got the 'mute' and 'camera off' buttons down pat!

Why did the GPS break up with the car?

It was tired of going in circles.

I've decided to become a personal trainer.

My fitness tracker just laughed at me.

Why was the computer at the bar?

It had a hard drive.

What did the computer say to its overworked user

You need a 'byte' to eat!

Why did the video editing software become so popular?

Because it knew how to 'cut' to the chase!

Why don't computers sleep?

Because they don't want to crash.

Why did the laptop join the football team?

It heard they needed a good 'keyboard' player!

Why do computers never fight?

They always accept the other's 'point of view'.

What did the laughing laptop say?

A Dell-ighted computer!

- -

Why did the gaming console apply for a job?

It heard the employer needed someone who could 'control' the situation!

- -

Why did the computer go to therapy?

It had too many 'windows' open!

- -

Why did the smartphone go to art class?

It wanted to learn how to 'draw' a call!

- -

Why was the GPS a good comedian?

It knew all the 'routes' to a joke!

Why did the cell phone wear glasses?

It lost all its contacts.

Why was the computer cold?

It left its Windows open!

Why did the fitness tracker go to the bank?

Because it wanted to 'step up' its savings!

Why did the smartphone go on a diet?

It had too many 'bytes'.

THE JOKE'S ON YOU, KIDDO!

A RESERVOIR OF WITTY COMEBACKS FOR THOSE SASSY LITTLE RASCALS.

Why don't fish play video games?

They get hooked too easily!

Â·

What's a fish's favorite exercise?

'Cod'iovascular workouts!

Â·

Why did the weightlifter bring a grill to the gym?

He heard about the importance of good 'bar-bells'!

What do you call a fish that's always late?

A 'tardy pike'!

Why don't campers play video games?

They can't find the right 'camping site'!

What do you call a power tool that's always late?

A 'drill-dally'!

Why was the traffic jam so sweet?

It had a lot of 'car-n syrup'!

Why did the gardener take up running?

He wanted to 'grow' his endurance!

What do you call a sneezing lawn mower?

'Achoo-t and Tidy'!

Why did the fitness enthusiast put a TV in his garden?

He wanted to do some 'channel surfing'!

Why don't campers like to play catch?

They can't 'pitch' a ball!

Why did the barbecue date the grill?

It couldn't resist the 'sizzling' personality!

What's a weightlifter's favorite type of coffee?

'Espresso-lift'!

Why did the fitness enthusiast bring a ladder to the gym?

Because he wanted to 'step up' his workout!

What did the flat tire say to the car?

'I can't 'wheel' with you anymore'!

Why don't online shoppers play football?

They prefer 'adding to cart' instead of 'catch'!

Why did the video game console go fishing?

It heard there were plenty of 'bites'!

What did the lawnmower say to the weed?

'You're really 'cutting' into my time'!

Why did the barbecue become a gardener?

It wanted to 'grill' some plants'!

. . . .

What did the power tool say to the screw?

'You really 'drill' me crazy'!

. . . .

Why did the coffee break up with the creamer?

It was tired of being 'mugged' all the time!

. . . .

What's a fitness expert's favorite type of coffee?

'Trim'presso!

. . . .

Why don't weightlifters play video games?

They can't handle the 'press'ure'!

What did the online shopping cart say to the athlete?

'I'm always 'checking out'!

What did the running shoes say to the jogger?

'We've got some 'sole' searching to do'!

Why did the traffic jam go to the beach?

It heard it was 'bumper' to bumper!

What's a hair loss patient's favorite gardening tool?

A 'bald hoe'!

Why did the fish start a family vacation business?

It was tired of being 'caught' at work'!

What did the flat tire say to the spare one?

'Inflate to be you'!

What's a jogger's favorite part of a computer?

The 'running' program !

What's a beach lover's favorite type of coffee?

'Brewed on the beach'!

What did the lawnmower say to the grass?

'I'm here to 'cut' you down to size'!

Why was the online shopper bad at sports?

He couldn't 'cartwheel'!

What did the power tool say to the nail?

'I'm just 'drill'ed to meet you'!

Why did the coffee sue the espresso?

It was 'grounds' for a lawsuit!

What's a runner's favorite type of music?

'Jog'n Roll'!

Why don't campers like to play video games?

They can't find the 'pause' button in nature!

What do you call a weightlifter who loves fishing?

A 'muscle fish'!

What's a beach lover's favorite technology device?

A 'sand-wich' maker!

Why did the online shopper a bad football player?

He kept trying to 'click and drag' the ball!

What did the running shoes say to the treadmill?

'We're just 'running' in circles here'!

Why did the fitness enthusiast put a TV in his garden?

He wanted to do some 'channel surfing'!

What do you call a power tool that loves to shop online?

A 'browser drill'!

What did the coffee break up with the creamer?

It was tired of being 'mugged' all the time!

. . . .

What's a hair loss patient's favorite day of the week?

'Bald'ay!

. . . .

What did the gardener go to the gym?

He wanted to 'rake' up the weights!

. . . .

PUNS

FROM

THE

FUTURE

FUTURISTIC PUNS THAT PROVE DAD JOKES ARE LIGHT YEARS AHEAD, IN THEIR OWN GALAXY.

Why don't computers ever take their hats off?

Because they have bad data hair.

Why don't robots ever get lost?

They always follow their byte!

What do you call a battery that doesn't charge?

Free of charge!

I thought I could predict the weather. Turns out I can't.

I rain into some problems.

. . . .

Why don't computers ever take their hats off?

Because they have bad data hair.

. . . .

Why don't robots ever get lost?

They always follow their byte!

. . . .

What do you call a battery that doesn't charge?

Free of charge!

. . . .

Why don't aliens get lost in space?

Because they always take the right space turn.

I tried to write a book about working from home.

But I couldn't find the write space.

· ·

Why did the smartphone go to school?

It wanted to have better cell service.

· ·

Why did the astronaut break up with their partner?

They said they needed space.

· ·

Why did the computer apply for a job?

It wanted to make some cache.

· ·

Why did the sun go to school?

It wanted to be brighter.

I started a job as a time traveler.

I'm already late on my first day.

· ⌢ · · · · · · · · · ·

Why did the computer go to therapy?

It had a hard drive.

· ⌢ · · · · · · · · · ·

What's a spaceman's favorite chocolate?

A Mars bar!

· ⌣ · · · · · · · · · ·

Why don't robots play hide and seek? Because

they always get found in the hardware.

· ⌢ · · · · · · · · · ·

Why did the astronaut bring a broom to space?

To clean up the stardust.

I thought about getting a job in renewable energy, but I didn't
want to wind up in the wrong place.

Why did the automated machine decide to go on a diet?
It had too many bytes.

Why was the computer cold at work?
It left its Windows open.

What do you call a talkative power outlet?
An electrifying conversationalist!

Why did the robot go to the beach?
It wanted to surf the net.

I tried to learn coding, but

I couldn't hack it.

. . . .

Why did the robot bring a backpack to work?

It wanted to pack up its data.

. . . .

Why don't computers get lost? They always

back up their data.

. . . .

Why did the smartphone go to the gym? It wanted

to get more 'app' muscle.

. . . .

Why did the robot refuse to play cards? It was

afraid of the chips.

Why do time travelers always carry a notepad? Because they *like to 'time' their travel.*

Why did the satellite go to school? To improve *its 'global' knowledge.*

I started a job in a space agency. It's out of this world, but *the commute is a nightmare.*

Why did the robot become a chef? It mastered *the art of cooking bytes.*

Why did the wind turbine go to music school? It wanted *to become a fan of rock.*

I attempted to pursue a career in space exploration, *but I couldn't find any space in my schedule.*

What term would you use for a robot who takes the stairs? *Elevator resistant!*

Why did the robot get a promotion? Because *it had all the right circuits.*

Why did the computer go to an art school? It wanted *to improve its graphics.*

Why did the robot go to the library? *It wanted to download a book.*

Why did the computer go to a concert? It wanted

to reboot its system.

I tried to become a climate scientist, but I was

snowed under with work.

I thought I'd become a digital nomad, but I couldn't

find the right 'site' to settle.

Why did the astronaut bring a pencil to space?

To draw the Milky Way.

Why do time travellers always carry a map?

So they don't go off course.

Why did the robot go to the gym?

It wanted to get more 'app' muscle.

· ︵ ︵ · · · · · · · · · · · · · · ·

I became a solar panel installer, but I couldn't

keep up with the current.

· ︵ ︵ · · · · · · · · · · · · · · ·

Why don't robots get sunburned? They always

wear a hard hat.

· ︵ ︵ · · · · · · · · · · · · · · ·

Why did the robot get a promotion? Because

it had all the right circuits.

· ︵ ︵ · · · · · · · · · · · · · · ·

Why did the robot go to an art school? It wanted

to improve its graphics.

How would you label a computer that sings?

A-Dell.

FAMILY

GATHERING

KILLERS

UNLEASH THESE JOKES AT GATHERINGS AND BE THE LIFE (OR DEATH) OF THE PARTY.

What was the turkey's message to the chicken on Thanksgiving?

'You're such a cluck up!'"

....  ....

I've become a chef specializing in home dinners.

My secret ingredient? The smoke detector

Why did the holiday lights say to the switch?

'You turn me on!'

I've started doing push-ups in the morning. I do two.

One when I fall out of bed, and the second when I push myself back in.

I've decided to become an interior decorator.

My preferred style? 'Laundry Chic'.

What did the mashed potatoes say to the gravy boat?

'You complete me!'

I'm starting a new exercise routine: I do a jog around the block

every time there's a commercial on TV. I'm still on the first lap.

Why don't politicians play chess? Because they

can't tell a king from a pawn.

I wanted to be a tour guide. My favorite place?

The path from the couch to the fridge.

Why was the Christmas tree bad at knitting?

It always dropped its needles.

I've decided to write a book.

It's called '101 Ways to Avoid Cleaning the House'.

What did the suitcase say to the flip-flops on vacation?

'I think we're going places!'

I've become an expert in gardening. My specialty?

Growing dust bunnies.

Why did the computer go to therapy? It had too many *Windows to cope with.*

I've decided to become a fitness guru. My favorite exercise? *Jumping to conclusions.*

Why don't newspapers ever go on vacation? Because they *have too many issues.*

I've decided to become a gardener. My green thumb? *It's mostly from the food coloring in the cookies.*

What did the laptop say to the mouse? *'You click with me.'*

I'm training for a marathon. So far, I've made it

from the couch to the fridge in record time.

Why did the calendar get promoted?

It had a lot of dates.

I've started a new diet where I eat in front of a mirror.

It's a great way to watch myself lose weight.

Why don't news reporters ever play hide and seek? Because

good luck hiding when your job is to be in the headlines.

I've decided to start a band. We only play one note,

but we play it really well.

What's orange and sounds like a parrot ?

A carrot.

· ·

I've decided to become a baker. I'm really

good at loafing around.

· ·

Why don't politicians make good gardeners? They're always

avoiding the grassroots.

· ·

I've become an expert in bird watching. Mostly I watch them

eat the seeds I was supposed to plant.

· ·

Why do we never play hide and seek with mountains? Because

they always peak.

How do you react when your nose goes on strike?

Pick-et.

- - -

I've decided to become a gardener. My specialty?

Growing dust bunnies.

- - -

What do you do when your clock is hungry?

Feed it time.

- - -

How would you refer to a bear with no socks on?

Bare-foot.

- - -

Patient: 'Doctor, I think I'm a bell.'

Doctor: 'Take these pills, and if they don't work, give me a ring!'

Why don't barbers make good secret agents?

They always split hairs.

How do you respond when your coffee is too loud?

You tell it to mellow out.

Why don't we ever see elephants hiding in trees? Because
they're really good at it.

Why don't we ever play cards in the jungle?

Too many cheetahs.

What did the Halloween pumpkin say to the pie?

'I've got a gut feeling about this.'

Why did the fish blush? Because

it saw the ocean's bottom.

What differentiates a feline from a comma? The feline possesses claws at

the end of its paws, and a comma is a brief pause at the end of a clause.

Why don't fish play basketball?

They're afraid of the net.

What was the reason for the cookie's visit to the physician?

It felt crummy.

Why did the belt get detained?

It involved the illicit handling of trousers.

BACKYARD

BAFFLERS

NATURE-INSPIRED DAD JOKES THAT'LL MAKE YOUR BACKYARD BBQ A MEMORABLE EVENT.

I tried going vegan, but then I realized

I'm more of a steakholder.

Why was the grass always giggling? Because

the sun tickled it every morning!

What did the steak say to the grill?

You're really heating things up!

I thought I'd try some backyard gardening, but it turned out
I couldn't even plant myself outside.

. . . .

I decided to become a weather forecaster. My forecast for today?
100% chance of me grilling!

. . . .

Why don't grills ever play hide and seek? Because
they always get fired up!

. . . .

I decided to become a chef specializing in health food, but then
I realized I can't even resist a good burger!

. . . .

What do you call a happy burger?
A bun-derful delight!

I considered becoming a comedian. My family said
they've never laughed harder.

Why did the slipper break up with the sock?
It felt too smothered!

I decided to start a home gym. I call it
'Running to the Grill'.

What did the sunshine say to the backyard?
You light up my life!

I thought about becoming a professional slipper tester because
I've mastered the art of loafing around.

What's the warmest state?

Sizzl-issippi!

I became a weatherman. Turns out, I'm not so good at predicting

the weather, but I'm great at making it rain burgers.

What do you call a burger that's been to space?

A flying saucer!

I tried starting a healthy diet, but then I realized

I'm just a well-seasoned carnivore.

I thought I'd try sunbathing, but it turns out

I'm more of a shady character.

What do you call a steak's favorite dance?

The Meatball!

I thought about becoming a slipper designer, but then

I realized I can't even design a simple salad!

Why did the grill go to therapy? Because

it had too many flare-ups!

I decided to become a burger flipper. My specialty?

Flip-flopping between diets.

What's a steak's favorite day of the week?

Fry-day!

I decided to take up gardening, but I couldn't
even grow tired of grilling!

Why did the slipper go to the party?
To have a ball!

I thought about being a weatherman. My forecast?
A downpour of dad jokes.

What does a cloud wear on a sunny day?
Sunscreen!

I became a chef, but my family prefers when I'm a comedian.
They say my jokes are well-done, unlike my steaks.

What's a slipper's favorite type of music?

Sole music!

· ·

If gaiety is the most effective cure, then

my jokes must be a health food.

· ·

What's a burger's favorite sport?

Patty-cake!

· ·

Why don't we make like a grill and

heat things up with some humor?

· ·

What does a grill say when it's ready?

I'm all fired up!

What's a slipper's favorite type of movie?

Footage films!

· ·

If you think steaks are high,

you should see my cholesterol!

· ·

What's a cloud's favorite exercise?

The sun salutation!

· ·

If you think I'm funny now, you should

see me flip a burger!

· ·

What do you do when a steak is in your path?

Take a meat-ing!

What's a slipper's favorite type of bread?

Toast!

You know, I've been known

to 'meat' my goals when it comes to grilling.

I inquired if my relatives had any interest in hearing a joke about the sun.

They said, 'Sure, let's have it light!'

My son asked me if I'd help him become a vegetarian.

I said, 'Sorry, I can't make that mis-steak.'

I shared with my spouse that I had certain thoughts about becoming a backyard clown.

She said, 'That's a clown-clusion I can get behind!'

Why was the lawn always nervous? Because
of all the grass-hoppers!

I told my doctor I feel like a pair of slippers. He said,
'Well, you do seem very comfortable with yourself!'

I thought about becoming a comedian. My family said
they've never laughed harder.

I told my doctor I feel like a steak, he said,
'Well, you do look well-done.'

My family asked me to make a joke about the weather. I said,
'I don't know, it might be too breezy for you.'

DINNER TABLE

DECEPTIONS

JOKES TO DISTRACT YOUR FAMILY FROM YOUR COOKING.

What's a football player's favorite part of the house?

The 'touchdownstairs'."

Where does a computer go to dance?

The 'disk-o'."

I've started a career as a house cleaner. You know what

they say, 'broomed' if you do, 'dusted' if you don't."

I decided to become a wall painter. My skills?

You could say I'm a pro at 'covering up' my mistakes.

. . . .

Why did the vacuum get promoted?

It really 'sucked up' to the boss.

. . . .

Why didn't the bread want to go grocery shopping?

It felt a little 'crusty'.

. . . .

What's the loudest pet you can get?

A 'trumpet'.

. . . .

What is the outcome of experiencing intense fear on two separate occasions?

You have a 'ghost' of a chance.

Why did the tomato turn red? Because
it saw the 'salad dressing'.

I thought about becoming a nutritionist,
but It was challenging for me to 'digest' all the given information.

Why did the cell phone go to therapy?
It had too many 'hang-ups'.

What's a cat's way of keeping law & order?
'Claw enforcement'.

Why did the cookie go to therapy?
It had 'crummy' self-esteem.

What's a tree's favorite drink?

'Root' beer.

Tried being a marriage counselor once. But

I couldn't figure out how to 'propose' the right solutions.

Why was the tomato blushing? Because

it 'saw' the salad dressing.

Why don't some couples go to the zoo? Because

they're afraid of the 'merry-go-round'.

What do you do when a chair breaks?

'Stand' up for it.

Why don't elephants use computers?

They're afraid of the 'mouse'.

I decided to become a sports commentator. But

I keep 'dropping the ball' on the live updates.

Why did the wall go to the doctor?

It just couldn't 'hold up' anymore.

What's a sprinter's favorite subject in school?

'Run-on sentences'.

Why did the banana seek medical attention?

It wasn't 'peeling' well.

I thought about being a chef, but my cooking is so bad,

even my pasta 'pasta-way'.

· ·

Why did the card get in trouble at school?

It kept 'playing' during class.

· ·

Why did the doughnut go to the dentist?

It needed a 'filling'.

· ·

The Ultimate Dad Joke Delivery Guide

Hey again! So, you've made it through the dad joke collection, and now you're probably itching to try them out on your family. But hold on just a second! A great dad joke is more than just the punchline; it's all about the delivery. That's where this bonus section comes in.

We've put together the ultimate dad joke delivery guide to help you elevate your joke-telling game to the next level. This guide will provide you with essential tips and tricks to ensure that your dad jokes land just right, every time. Remember, it's all about having fun and making people laugh, so let's get started!

≈ TIMING IS EVERYTHING ≈

1

Wait for the Perfect Moment: When someone asks, "What's the time?" don't waste the opportunity to say, "Time to tell a dad joke!" They'll never see it coming.

2

Interrupt with Style: Got a punchline that just can't wait? Burst into a conversation like the Kool-Aid Man with your joke – your family will adore your impeccable timing.

3

Use Awkward Silences: When everyone's quiet and unsure what to say, it's your cue to swoop in and save the day with a dad joke. They'll thank you later.

≋ THE ART OF THE EYE ROLL ≋

1

Perfect Your Technique: For maximum effect, roll your eyes so hard they might get stuck. This way, everyone knows you're committed to the joke.

2

Timing Matters: Eye roll too soon, and you'll spoil the punchline. Wait too long, and the moment's gone. Practice makes perfect, so keep rolling those eyes.

3

Encourage Participation: Get the whole family in on the eye-rolling action! It's like synchronized swimming, but on dry land and with 100% more sarcasm.

≈ CONFIDENCE IS KEY ≈

1

Own Your Puns: When delivering a dad joke, puff your chest, stand tall, and remember - you're the king of puns. Embrace your inner Shakespeare.

2

Boldly Ignore Doubters: Naysayers gonna naysay. Don't let them dull your sparkle. With each eye roll and groan, remember - you're the dad joke superhero.

3

Practice on Pets: Rehearse your jokes on Fido or Fluffy. They're non-judgmental, and their silence is a sign of pure admiration for your dad joke mastery.

Cover illustration by The Gratitude Library.

Book design by The Gratitude Library.

First Edition: May 2023

Made in United States
Troutdale, OR
06/08/2023

10509012R10065